dali

dali

Text and layout design by
JACQUES DOPAGNE

LEON AMIEL PUBLISHER
NEW YORK

Published by
LEON AMIEL PUBLISHER
NEW YORK
ISBN Number 8148-0590-6
© 1974 ADAGP
Printed in Italy

"Do you think in three years you will have forgotten this painting?" Dali asked Gala one day as he showed her the famous "soft watches" in the *Persistence of Memory* (59).

"No one who has seen this painting will ever forget it," Gala answered.

Gala was right. This picture, like most of Dali's works, is an unforgettable spectacle. For many people, however, it is Dali himself who provides the spectacle, not his painting. His pictorial work plays a secondary role or, more precisely, is reduced to a sort of constantly revolving stage set that serves as a background against which Dali interprets his own role with dazzling virtuosity. In each of his appearances he looks like a great eccentric who takes pleasure in saying the most provocative things and making the most scandalous gestures. In short, the public is fascinated more by his conjuring tricks than by his painting. But this ambiguity, which is obviously intentional, is carried off with a brilliance that verges on genius, and Dali seems to have made it the rule that governs his life, or at least his public life. In this way he undoubtedly achieves his goal, namely, at one and the same time to mystify, and to make himself noticed by, the greatest possible number of onlookers. In effect, he encourages them to see his extravagances as simple buffoonery and to think of his painterly gifts as an outgrowth of his talent as a prestidigitator. His painting then becomes no more than one of the accessories he uses as a magician or, if one prefers, as a dandy. With the absurd insolence of an "anachronistic hidalgo," he upgrades this dandyism to a genuinely philosophical level. For example, Dali unhesitatingly asserts: "Every time someone dies, it's Jules Verne's fault. He's the one who's responsible for trips into interplanetary space, which are only good for boyscouts and people who like underwater fishing. Just think: if the enormous sums swallowed up by space travel were invested in biological research, no one would die any more on our planet. And so, I repeat, every time someone dies, it's Jules Verne's fault."

Dali is also the man who, when he stepped off the boat that brought him to New York fot the first time in 1934, approached the awaiting journalists waving an eight feet long stick of bread that he had asked the ship's baker to prepare specially for him. And it was also Dali who, another day, appeared in

"Bon jour chère amie!"

front of a stupefied public wearing a tuxedo upon which a number of imitation flies had been pinned. Dali also once went on a lecture tour dressed in a diving suit; when he arrived at the Sorbonne, he noisily clambered out of a Rolls-Royce that was filled with cauliflowers.

It would be easy to quote similar examples of Dali's behavior, not to mention the countless declarations and statements of all kinds that Dali has never been afraid of making, whether on radio and television or in other media, concerning the magnetic characteristics of his moustache or the "stereoscopic" happiness that he says he has experienced at the Perpignan train station. His acts as well as his words have certainly won Dali a reputation that, although international, is nonetheless based on a vast misunderstanding. The truth is that this reputation is misleading and many people have been, and still are, deceived by it, even critics, who unfortunately are not always able to distinguish between what is factitious and what is serious. Dali himself, particularly in these last few years, has begun to deplore this misunderstanding; indeed, to the point where he thought it necessary to specify: "When people finally pay attention to my work, they will see that my painting is like an iceberg that shows only one tenth of its volume." Sometimes, on the other hand, Dali accepts this misunderstanding: "How can you expect my enemies, my friends and the general public to understand the meaning of the images that rise up in me and that I transcribe in my paintings when I myself, who *create* them, do not understand them either."

However it may be, the pictorial work accomplished by Dali is enormous, a fact that many people are not sufficiently aware of. From a qualitative as from a quantitative point of view, it dominates, along with Picasso's, the art of the twentieth century. Dali is literally *possessed* by the spirit of painting: painting for him is not the simple exploitation of his gifts, even though those gifts are as brilliant as they are natural. In truth, possession is tantamount to anguish, and Dali knows this better than anyone. He writes: "The most well-kept secret is that the most famous painter in the world, that is, myself, still doesn't know to go about painting. Oh, if only I weren't afraid to paint!"

Make no mistake about it: beneath the hyperbolic aspect of this quip is hidden the anguish of creation. The clowning and buffoonery that Dali uses to amuse some and exasperate others are a screen masking a creator of genius, a creator who is also a tireless worker who never stops searching. "If you refuse to study anatomy, the art of drawing and perspective, the mathematics of aesthetics and the science of colors, allow me to tell you that it's more a sign of laziness than of genius." There is no lack of evidence concerning Dali's rage to work, the passionate ardor that already marked his first attempts at painting during his early adolescence, how he would shut himself up for hours in his workshop and relieve his extreme nervous tension by humming monotonously and continuously like a bee buzzing until finally he would come out after having finished the two or three pictures he had set himsel as that day's task. It is often related how, after he met the woman who was to become his wife, Gala (who, "the ever-watchful," has remained unfailingly near to him), he secluded himself with her in a small hotel on the Côte d'Azur where he stayed two months without leaving his room in a snug, clammy atmosphere lit only by an electric light, the shutters closed, that favored the subconscious resurgence of a flood of intrauterine memories. The point of this was to work on his famous painting *The Invisible Man* and to prepare the series that stemmed from it: *Profanation of the Host* (13), *The Great Masturbator* (21), *The First*

Days of Spring (15 and 16), to name only a few. Similarly, it took him no less than six months to finish *The Breadbasket* (5), a still-life to which he patiently applied himself with all the meticulous and at the same feverish precision of the great masters of Dutch painting. Such examples abound in Dali's life and bear witness to the ascetism that this frenetic actor can submit himself to whenever he is seized by the imperious desire to complete a painting well.

In addition, the more attentively one analyzes Dali's writings and statements, however extravagant or crazy they may seem, the keener one's insight into his painting grows. It becomes easier to see the technical accomplishments, whether they are of a plastic, graphic, chromatic or rhythmic order etc., and the truth stands out more and more vividly: what Dali seeks above all is the cult of the image for the image's sake or, more precisely, the cult of a new image that would be "like a living, redoubled nature." The impact and intensity of the message that is communicated depend on how this image is treated, on the precision and minuteness of detail with which it is rendered, on its "optical reality" and "naturally supernatural" light.

In any case, it is in this sense that we should take the exhibition of "Peintres Pompiers" that

Dali organized with much pomp in 1967 at the Hotel Meurice in Paris. This was intended to be his personal response to the double current of Op and Pop Art. He would undoubtedly react in the same way today in 1974 with respect to Photo-Realism and Conceptual Art, and it is likely he would repeat what he said then: "I would like it to be known that after Op and Pop Art it will be the turn of Art Pompier quantified by everything of any importance that has happened in that movement as well as by all the experiences, even the most insane, of that grandiose tragedy that can be called Modern Art."

Although this statement, to a certain degree, can be justified, this is not the place to discuss it. Inevitably the question will be raised as to why Dali needs to rely on so many theatrical sets and histrionic effects. Why so many manifestations that are outside of or alien to his work, so many provocative diatribes, so many disconcerting and even unpleasant statements about his own person and his particular genius? Certainly one can object to his having written: "Me, I'm a retarded polymorphic pervert with anarchizing tendencies... I am destined to save nothing less than painting from the great void of modern art..." But one

can also approve of him for having said: "Don't worry about trying to be modern for that's the one thing that, no matter what you do, you unfortunately can't avoid being." And one can understand him perfectly when he observes: "I am penetrating more and more into the magic of the universe." (53, 68, 69, 74, 75).

In any case, it would be an error to try to dissociate Dali as an artist from Dali as a theatrical personage. However exasperating it may be, Dali never strikes an attitude for simple reasons of publicity, or at least for that purpose alone. Things are more complex. Dali has need of continual excitement, a stimulation that is absolutely indispensable to his painterly temperament, and which he finds, precisely, in the exhibitionism he indulges in whenever he has an audience. There is no doubt that some of his "exhibitions" laid the groundwork for the acceptance of his pictures, especially those that were the most bizarre or in advance of their time, since their audacity did not shock a public that saw them as being illustrations of a sort of modern psychodrama. It was in this way that Dali undertook the exploration of his most secret, and thus most powerful, phantasms (death, eroticism, childhood, space, time, matter, science, etc.). Today, when many artists conceal their weakness under the banner of some school or group, Dali, on the other hand, completely independent, has developed a method that is unique of its kind whose purpose is to trigger the release of a maximum of creative energy. He himself refers to it as a method of "critical paranoia," that is, a spontaneous process "of irrational knowledge founded on the critical and interpretative association of delirious phenomena."

As can be seen, Dali is very explicit. He does not want any ambiguity to exist in this respect. As to his attitude concerning the use of drugs as a stimulus for artistic creation, here is what Timothy Leary, the prophet of LSD, had to say: "Dali is the only LSD painter who doesn't need LSD." And Dali goes on to say: "This is normal for anyone who (like myself) seeks to render with the greatest possible precision the images of concrete irrationality. On the other hand, there is nothing in the world that bores me more than to have to listen to people who insist on speaking about their dreams and hallucinations, neither of which they're capable of really evoking. The eye is a miraculous thing but you have to know how to use it as I did mine by turning it into a soft, psychedelic camera. I can stimulate my eye into taking pictures not of external things but of the inner visions of my thought. Those who can provoke these visions at will never have to come in contact with the sadness of everyday reality and can give free rein to the paranoiac magic of their hallucinations... I never took drugs because I *am* drugs. I don't have to speak about my hallucinations, I bring them into being. Take me, *I am the drug,* take me, I'm hallucinogenic."

Statements like this obviously reveal all of Dali's personality. But one must be careful not to conclude that his personality is simple. Despite the extreme, superindividualized character of Dali's public manifestations, the real Dali lies beneath them and is made up of many more facets than meet the eye. Indeed, it is possible to be "whole" without being "all of a piece." This is precisely what is shown by a remarkable study that was written by Doctor P. Rouméguère and published in "Dali par Dali de Draeger" in 1970. It is entitled "Cosmic Dali or the Royal Path of Access to the Dalinian Universe." In particular, the psychiatrist writes: "Certainly there is a Dali case, a psychopathological case. But if the public paid more attention to its real message and less to the extravagances that surround it, it would discover an unknown, secret and fascinating Dali, a side of Dali that is actually as public and visible as the other because both express themselves in function of each other." These few lines from the introduction are immediately followed by further observations that are much more precise and revelatory: "When Dali was a small child he got off to a very, very bad start in life on account of a veritable *hallucinogenic* series of objective chances that irrevocably conditioned his imagination and sensibility...

"It so happened that three years before Dali was born another small Dali, seven years old, died from meningitis. It also so happened that Dali was a *mirror image* of the other, they resembled each other like twins. His unhappy parents, desperately attached to the first Dali, committed the crime of giving the new Dali the same first name as the other had had. In the parent's room, in that place that was so terrible *charged,* filled with the presence of mysterious activities... in that sacred place of ambivalence, high up on the wall could be seen, as if enthroned, a large photograph of the dead Dali, double and twin of the other, that is, of the small (living) Dali who looked at the photo of his brother, fascinated by everything he heard about him from his parents. Yet another extraordinary coincidence was that next to the dead Dali, as if to keep him company, Dali's father, despite the fact that the was an atheist, a sectarian, fanatic and unconditional spirit, had placed the image of another cadaver, the reproduction of a Crucified Christ painted by Velasquez! It is simply not thinkable that Dali's mother, his nurse Lucia or some other servant did not secretly explain to him that his dead brother had *ascended* even higher toward the celestial kingdom where the Crucified One was waiting for him...

"There was still another series of incredible and absurd coincidences: the first name of his atheist father *Salvador,* was also Christ's and was given to the first small Dali as well as to the second. This derisory use of the name of Saviour had a morbid, obsessive effect on the (new) small Dali, sole survivor of this true and crazy story. Were not these four saviours—dead, mortifying, mortified—a little bit too much to take for a fresh, young consciousness that was just opening up to the world and to life?"

And Doctor Rouméguère continues: "During these first years in which sensibility, emotion and imagination work to build character and *physical structure* that will act as a support and guiding model for all present and future behavior, for all future emotional, intellectual and aesthetic

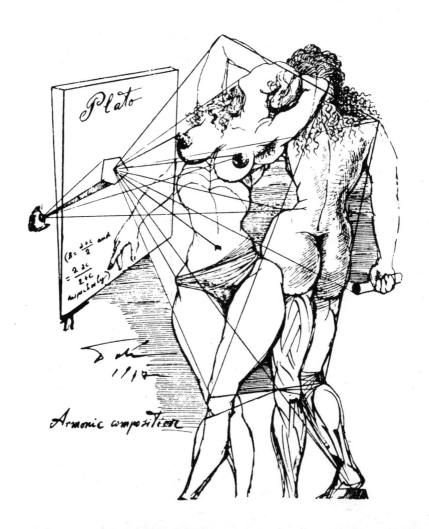

Plato

$(B = \frac{a+c}{2}$ and
$= \frac{2\,ac}{2+c}$
$respective(y)$

Armonic composition

categories, the destiny of the little Salvador IV was caught in this play of mirrors, of mirages, of reflections and overlapping illusions that rebounded between the four Salvadors, living and dead... (86) Among all these dead, who was he? A substitute, a surrogate, someone condemned to death but not yet dead? He certainly did not possess his own firm, solid reality but was a replica, a double, an absence; his existence seemed blurred, unreal, imaginary, soft, and its indecisive, ambiguous, ambivalent and polyvalent contours merged with those of the outer world... Salvador IV was also a prodigious *psychic athlete* equipped with brilliant and exceptional abilities, both in terms of quality and quantity."

These lines by Doctor Rouméguère throw a harsh light on the profound personality of Dali. They also provide a key that makes it that much easier to understand his behavior. Everything can be explained and falls into place, both Dali as a social personage as well as Dali as a painter. According to this masterly analysis, Dali's life cannot but be divided into three clearly characteristic periods: Dali *before* Gala until 1929, Dali *and* Gala until 1941 and after that *Gala-Dali,* which was how the painter signed all of his pictures from then on, discovering in this way for himself a truth that psychologists have long been familiar with: "the name is the person."

Given these conditions, what then was Dali's childhood? There seems to be no doubt that he was a child prodigy, but he also was a child whom fatality had deprived of his real personality. The result of this was, of course, his deep-seated exhibitionism, his dandyism, his urge for depersonalization, which explains the first period in his painting: *The Aesthetics of the Soft and the Conquest of the Irrational.* It was a perilous conquest and more than once his reason nearly foundered in its abysses.

As a young man Dali first studied at the muncipal school of Figueras. With a few friends he started a review called Studium which was printed as a sign of revolt on ordinary wrapping paper. Dali wrote several virulent articles for it on the "Great Masters of Painting." At the age of seventeen he enrolled in the School of Fine Arts in Madrid where he immediately distinguished himself by systematically doing the contrary of everyone else. When he was asked to draw a statue of the Virgin from a model, he handed his scandalized professor the image of a pair of scales. Or he made a bet that he could paint a picture without touching the canvas with his brush. He won the bet by dripping color on the canvas from about a yard away, creating fantastic stains. Or else, refusing to answer the questions his examiners asked him, he pretended he was more intelligent and more competent than all of them put together. The same style, naturally, was apparent in his dress: he wore short pants with garters, a big black felt cap that was entirely covered with hairs and a floor-length cape. He created so many scandals and provocations that he was finally expelled from the School of Fine Arts for misconduct. His best friends at the time were Federico Garcia Lorca and Luis Buñuel.

Salvador Dali's first pictures were no more than experiences at the start. He was not only seeking to find himself but also to find the style of painting that would be unmistakably his own. After a few Impressionist (1) and Cubist attempts in which his fondness for the unusual was already apparent, he undertook more original works by gluing pebbles and pieces of driftwood he had found on Catalan beaches on the canvas. An exhibition of these works as well as of a few others such as *The Breadbasket* (5) that took place at the Dalmau Gallery in Barcelona, in addition to the stage sets that he designed for

Lorca's play *Mariana Pineda,* received an unexpectedly favorable press. But far from moderating or calming his temperament, this success only increased Dali's anticonformism. Together with Buñuel he wrote letters full of insults to the most famous Spanish personalities and officials. On the same burst of inspiration and again in collaboration with his friend Buñuel, Dali wrote the script for the famous film *Un Chien Andalou.* When the film came out in Paris at Studio 28 it caused a scandal that was perfectly in accord with the measure of their ambitions. For instance, the critic Eugenio Montès concluded: "Dali and Buñuel have just taken up a position that is without any doubt on the outside of what is called good taste, of what is pretty, agreeable and superficial, in short, of those qualities that are specifically French."

In the wake of this the Surrealist movement could do no more than accept Dali as a choice recruit. "It cannot be denied," wrote André Breton, "that the poetic and visionary content of these pictures has a density and an extraordinary explosive force." Dali perfectly assimilated the fundamental ideas of Surrealism which he interpreted in his own way, developing them to a point of paroxysm. The memory of his early childhood haunted him more than ever and he exploited this vein more than anyone before him had dared to do (10, 14, 25, 31, 32, 37, 51, 61, 62, 85). His technical skill was equal to the violence he expressed. In each of his pictures, thanks to a sort of mental anamorphosis constantly on the alert, as well as to a dazzling mastery of line, color and perspective, he succeeded in obtaining a maximum of effect.

The target of his violence was both his former identification with a dead person as well as parental authority which he attacked with unprecedented fury *(The Old Age of William Tell,* (12), *The Hand,* (19), and especially the famous *Enigma of William Tell,* (37), which along with *Lugubrious Games* (10) is undoubtedly one of Dali's most dramatic works. The image he gave of himself or rather of his psychosis had to do most frequently with rotting corpses eaten by worms and insects, devoured by excrescences of soft flesh, held up by bony structures that were also soft. In the Dalinian aesthetic of that time everything became ineluctably soft, including sexual obsessions, which also were translated most of the time by soft turgescences. All of his forms grew soft as if under the effect of an epidemic. Their monstrous elongations were the obvious result of methodically carried out hallucinogenic intoxications. How did Dali keep from falling into a state of pure and simple madness? A thin thread of reason kept him alive; a small dose of reality served as a support. In this way, thanks to an arsenal of crutches, he managed at all costs to keep the immense limp form that threatened him upright (32» For this limp form was precisely what he had to conquer, all the more so in that it was directly related to the dead person that had been imposed upon him and that he had to refuse with all his strength, and overcome. Conquering death in fact has always been, and will always be, the central problem of Dali's life. "Death is very important to me," Dali confessed in one of his books. "Next to eroticism it's the subject that interests me the most."

It was at this moment that, according to Doctor Rouméguère, the *therapeutic* miracle took place: Gala! When she became a part of Dali's life, imagination was transformed into reality, for Gala suddenly broke the evil mirror. Dali's exhausting voyage through the world of appearances was now over. Dali now *saw himself* in Gala. She gave him an image of himself that he could identify with and that soothed his narcissistic tendencies. From now on he no longer related himself to his dead twin but, so to speak, to his living twin.

Dali's work now took another direction or, rather, its development was governed by new polarities. There were no more interdicts, nothing that Dali did not dare. Dali took advantage of this new freedom to delve into all of his phobias and obsessions and to turn them to his advantage. He knew that Gala was next to him, a vigilant and lucid counsellor; she alone was capable of putting a check on the terrible games that engaged his subconscious and his intellect. Once Dali had written: "Since my earliest childhood I have gotten into the vicious habit of thinking of myself and acting like the contrary of ordinary mortals." Now, however, the way was open for him to attempt to exorcize this childhood. Many of his pictures are, in this respect, very meaningful, for in them, precisely, he portrayed himself as a child confronted by forces that went beyond him. This is especially evident in *The First Days of Spring*. It is a photo of Dali himself that can be seen in the small frame in the center of the composition, withness and victim at one and the same time of an hallucinatory erotic ballet (15). But it stands out above all in *The Ghost of Sex Appeal* (62) in which a small boy (another

version of Dali as a child) dressed in a sailor's costume looks with bewilderment at a monstrous and instable apparition of female sexuality. The same holds true for *Paranoiac-Astral Image* (38) in which Dali, still dressed in a sailor's costume, has an imaginary encounter with Gala, who is alone with him in a boat washed up on the beach of Rosas; the picture is subtitled *False Memory*. Still the same can be said for another picture entitled *Old Age, Adolescence, Infancy* (51) in which the same small boy is enchased and as if imprisoned in the pictorial substance of one of the three symbolic faces. And finally, although it is a later work, the famous *Hallucinogenic Toreador* (86) in which the child in the sailor's costume is depicted again, terrorized this time by the recollection of all the dead Salvadors with whom he had been coupled.

Almost all of Dali's work is thus progressively marked by reference points and reminiscences. Each time we feel how the painter desired to express both the incantatory and obsessional characteristics of his experience. For example, in *The Weaning of Furniture Nutrition* (31) we see the heavy, swollen figure of a woman seated on the beach. She is intersected by the edge of a bedside table whose volume, besides, is absorbed by another smaller bedside table. Far from being the product of chance, the female figure represents Lucia the nurse. It is thus logical for her to be called "a comestible piece of furniture;" the smaller bedside table then can logically be seen as her child whom she is feeding. This woman turns up several times in Dali's work (39, 51). This theme is treated in the same way as that of the pianos, that is, it is successively an object of abhorrence or of lyrical attraction (23, 42, 43).

The same applies to the theme of the skulls which, depending on the period, are hard or soft, as well as to the watches, which may be soft or "desintegrated" (59, 60) but invariably are revelatory of a Dali subject to the cosmic anguish of "space-time."

As for Gala, his wife and his "twin," it would be an understatement to say that she forms one of the thematic elements of Dali's work. She is the very substance on which his work is built; she is the ends and means merged together. Especially starting in 1941, Dali depicts Gala in a thousand and one ways, as a saint, an odalisk, a madonna, a magician. Dali sees her in a way that is as inexhaustible as his imagination. And even if, in some paintings or in some series of paintings, her presence is more difficult to detect, for instance in the famed *Soft Construction with Dried Boiled Beans* (35) which Dali subtitled *Premonition of the Spanish Civil War,* an attentive examination makes it possible to discern this presence which, although invisible, is nonetheless real: The piece of furniture that supports this apocalyptic construction, the famous *meuble-aliment,* is intact this time, hermetically closed and obviously laden with an ent ire mechanism of saving and redemptive forces.

When Dali returned from the United States at the end of the Second World War, he took up residence again at Cadaquès and announced with much fanfare that he was going to give his work a new meaning, a meaning that would be radically opposed to the one it had had until then.   Dali asserted that he had been touched by Grace and was returning to "vertical Spanish mysticism."   He who in the past had uttered so many blasphemies and drawn his inspiration from the most provocative sacrileges was now interested in only one thing: expressing his religious fervor. He did this in the purest traditional way while at the same time he showed a sudden attachment to the established values of traditional Art.   He became the ardent standard-bearer of the classical masters. "Before

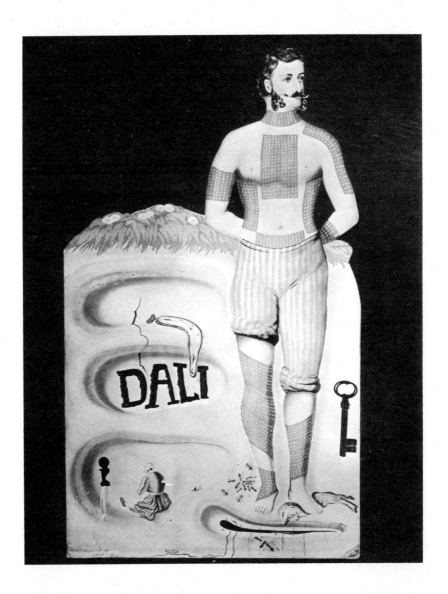

falling asleep," he declared, "instead of rubbing my hands I embrace them with a very pure joy while I say to myself that the Universe is a very insignificant thing when compared to the perfection of a forehead painted by Raphael." In reality, and regardless of the quality of his faith, it did not take long for the public to realize that the neophyte Dali had come up with nothing less than a new programm of provocation. Once again he diconcerted the bystanders. At the same time he aroused the hostility of a few painters and critics, the more or less clairvoyant proselytes of the new avant-garde.

Since then Dali has continued to play brilliantly his role as a defender of the throne and altar, of the sword and the aspersorium. Can it be said that his recent manner contains as much subversive power as was evident in the past? The question may be asket. And the time is remote as well when Dali wrote such stunning aphorisms as: "Beauty is only the sum of the consciousness of our perversions" or "Eroticism is the monarchical principle that cybernetically flows in the molecular structures of DNA." Or when he painted such pictures as *Young Virgin Auto-sodomized by her Own Chastity* (66) or *The Great Masturbator* (21). Certainly the mystical-nuclear and political-scientific kind of painting he does today shows breath-taking technical accomplishments. The huge picture that he entitled *Discovery of America by Christopher Columbus* (71, 72, 73, 74) as well as *Velasquez* (75), *Dionysius* (82) and a few others are pictorial masterworks, whatever their lack of lyrical inspiration may be. Despite all the whims, caprices, contradictions and turnabouts of his behavior and intelligence, it cannot be denied that Dali has remained unshakably faithful to certain principles. He founded his mythology on a single woman, Gala, and on a single place, Port Lligat. He has always treated the same fundamental themes, which are as central to his work today as they were to his work in the past. And he continues to exalt the supremacy of the imagination with the same convincing effectiveness. In truth, there have been few men who have exalted the imagination with as much energy and rigor.

Paradoxically, the artist who puts the most emphasis on delirium has never undertaken anything that is not based on some idea that has been carefully prepared in advance. Thus there is not a single painting by this master that does not have its place and very precise meaning in the general context of his work. However, it is of course necessary to know how to discover this secret order.

Translated by
Wade Stevenson

1904

Birth at Figueras (Spain) on May 11. Dali's father is a notary.

1914-1918

Dali studies with the Maristes Brothers at Figueras.

1918-1919

Influence of nineteenth-century Spanish painters, of the Impressionists and the Pointillists.

1919

Together with a few friends Dali founds the review *Studium.*

1920

He discovers the Italian Futurists.

1921-1922

He attends the School of Fine Arts in Madrid and meets Luis Buñuel and Federico Garcia Lorca. He exhibits eight of his first paintings at the Dalmau Gallery.

1923

He discovers the Italian *metaphysical painters* Chirico and Carlo Carrà. He is expelled from the School of Fine Arts for misconduct.

1924

For political reasons he is imprisoned for a few days at Figueras and Gerona. He illustrates *Les Bruixes de Llers* by C. Fages de Climent.

1925

First one-man show at the Dalmau Gallery (17 paintings and 5 drawings). Dali's name begins to become known. He is considered as the leader of the young Catalan painters.

1927

New exhibition at the Dalmau Gallery (20 paintings, 7 drawings). He contributes regularly to many newspapers and art reviews. First trip to Paris.

1928

Second trip to Paris. He meets Picasso and André Breton. He sees much of the Surrealists and soon is part of the group. A few of his works are exhibited for the first time in the United States at the Carnegie Institute in Pittsburg.

1928

He does a series of collages that show the influence of Max Ernst, Miró, Arp and other contemporary artists. Gala and Paul Eluard visit Dali at Cadaquès.

1929

First exhibition in Paris at the Galerie Goeman (11 paintings). Gala and Paul Eluard visit him a second time at Cadaquès in the company of René Char. Dali is more and more fascinated by Gala. He decides that she will become his wife. The film *Un Chien Andalou* comes out in Paris and causes an enormous scandal.

1930

He writes and illustrates *The Visible Woman* which he dedicates to Gala. He paints *The Great Masturbator* and participates in the illustrations of the *Immaculate Conception* by Paul Eluard and André Breton. He works on another project with Buñuel. Their new film *L'Age d'Or* also gives rise to a scandal.

1931

8 paintings and 2 drawings by Dali are among the works exhibited at the *Wadsworth Atheneum* in Hartford, Connecticut. He writes *Love and Memory.*

1932

His picture *Persistence of*

Memory is exhibited in New York at Julien Lévy's.

1933

Another exhibition at Julien Lévy's of 26 large paintings. Dali is very preoccupied by the legend of William Tell and by Millet's the *Angelus*. He explains the reasons for this fascination in the review the *Minotaure*. His first Surrealist works are exhibited in Barcelona at the Gallery of Catalan Arts.

1934

First exhibition in London at the Zwemmer Gallery (16 paintings, 20 drawings, 17 engravings). Breaks with André Breton and leaves the Surrealist group. He illustrates the *Chants de Maldoror* by Lautréamont.

1935

Contributes to the *Cahiers d'Art* with *Honor to the Object*. He paints the *Instant Figures* that appear to him on the beach of Rosas (Spain). He develops his famous *method of critical paranoia* which he explains in the *Conquest of the Irrational*.

1936

He is supported financially by the English patron of the arts Edward F.W. James, for whom Dali executes several important paintings most of which were destroyed by the Nazis.

1937

Trip to Italy. Dali's interest goes toward the Renaissance and Baroque painters.

1938

Travels through Europe. Meets Sigmund Freud whose portrait he paints.

1939

Dali stages his ballet *Bacchanal* at the Metropolitan Opera House in New York.

1940

Fleeing the German invasion, Dali leaves Europe and takes refuge in the United States.

1941-1942

First important retrospective exhibition at the Museum of Modern Art in New York (43 paintings and 17 drawings). This retrospective is then shown in eight large American cities. Dali becomes very famous in the United States. He publishes *The Secret Life* of Salvador Dali.

1943

Exhibition of 29 pictures at M. Knoedler and Co. in New York. Dali decorates Helena Rubinstein's new apartment.

1944-1946

He illustrates several books including *Fantastic Memories* and *Labyrinth* by M. Sandoz, Macbeth, Montaigne's *Essays* and the *Autobiography of B. Cellini*.

1948

Dali returns to Port Lligat. He begins to direct his art in the sense of Religion and of a new Classicism.

1949

He paints *The Madonna of Port Lligat*. He receives the Pope's approval for this work.

1951

Dali publishes his *Mystical Manifesto*. In it he explains his ideas about what he calls "nuclear Art."

1952

He does 102 illustrations for Dante's *Divine Comedy*.

1954

He publishes *Dali Mous-*

taches. Large retrospective in Rome (24 oils, 17 drawings and the 102 watercolors of *The Divine Comedy*. With Robert Descharnes he begins work on a film entitled: *The Prodigious History of the Lace-Worker and the Rhinoceros*.

1956

Retrospective at Knokke le Zoute, Belgium (34 oils, 48 drawings and watercolors). It is the first exhibition that he does not directly supervise himself. He publishes *The Cuckolds of Old Modern Art*.

1957-1959

Dali creates some of his major works: *Santiago El Grande* and the *Discovery of America by Christopher Columbus*, among others.

1961

Publication of the *Secret Life of Salvador Dali*. The *Ballet of Gala*, written by Dali and for which he designed the costumes, is performed in Venice. He paints the famed picture the *Ecumenical Council*.

1962

Dali completes *The Battle of Tetouan*.

1963

Publication of the *Tragic Myth of Millet's Angelus*.

1964

Large retrospective in Tokyo. Publication of *Diary of a Genius*.

1965

Dali illustrates the Bible. He executes his first large sculpture *Bust of Dante* and completes one of his masterworks: *The Apotheosis of the Dollar*.

1966

Very important retrospective at the Gallery of Modern Art in New York. Dali publishes his *Open Letter to Salvador Dali*.

1967

Dali organizes his *Homage to Meissonier* and to the *Peintres Pompiers* (Hotel Meurice, Paris). This exhibition includes his famous picture *Tuna Fishing*. He illustrates poems by Guillaume Apollinaire and Mao Tse Tung and supervises a new edition of the Bible he illustrated.

1968

He writes and publishes *Dali de Draeger*. He illustrates Ronsard and Sade.

1969

He illustrates *Erotic Metamorphoses*, *Faust*, *Tristan and Isolde* and *Carmen*. He paints the picture *The Hallucinogenic Toreador*.

1970

Inauguration of the Dali Museum at Figueras (Spain). Publication of *Dali by Dali*. Large retrospective at the Boysman van Beuningen Museum in Rotterdam.

1971

Inauguration of the Dali Museum in Cleveland (Ohio). Retrospective at Baden-Baden (Germany). He illustrates André Malraux's book *Roi, Je T'Attends à Babylone*. The series of engravings entitled *Homage to Dürer* is exhibited at Visions Nouvelles in Paris.

1972

First exhibition of three-dimensional paintings and holograms at the Knoedler Gallery in New York. Dali selects many of his works that were in the reserves of the Prado for the Dali Museum in Figueras.

LIST OF PLATES

PLANCHES

PLATES

1
Cadaquès
1923

2　Cadaquès　1923

4
La Fille de l'Ampurdan
1926
Girl with Curls

3   Femme couchée. 1926. Reclining Woman.

5   La Corbeille de pain. 1926. The Basket of Bread.

6
Appareil et Main
1927
Apparatus and Hand

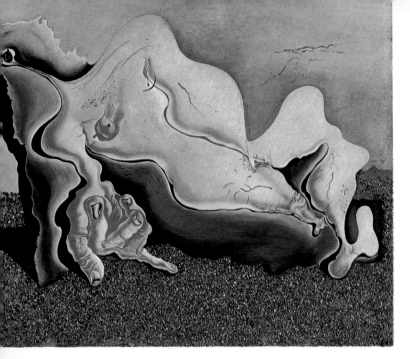

7 Beigneuse (sic). 1928.

8
Les Plaisirs
illuminés
1929
The Illuminated
Pleasures

9
L'ombre de
la nuit s'avance
1931
Shades of Night
Descending

10
Jeux lugubres
détail
1929
Lugubrious Games

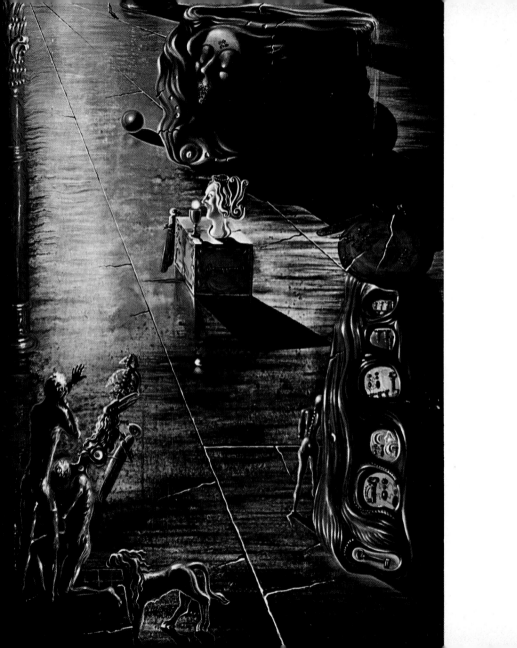

11
La Fontaine
1928
The Fountain

12 La Vieillesse de Guillaume Tell. 1931. The Old Age of William Tell.

13   14
Profanation de l'hostie
détail et ensemble
1929
Profanation of the Host

15   16
Les Premiers Jours du printemps
détail et ensemble
1929
The First Days of Spring

17   Bureaucrate moyen. détail. 1930. The Average Bureaucrat.

18   Le Rêve. 1932. The Dream.

19 La Main. 1930. The Hand.

21 Le Grand Masturbateur. 1929. The Great Masturbator.

22   Œufs sur le plat sans le plat. 1932.

23
Six Apparitions
de Lénine sur
un pianoforte
1931
Six Apparitions of
Lenin on a Piano

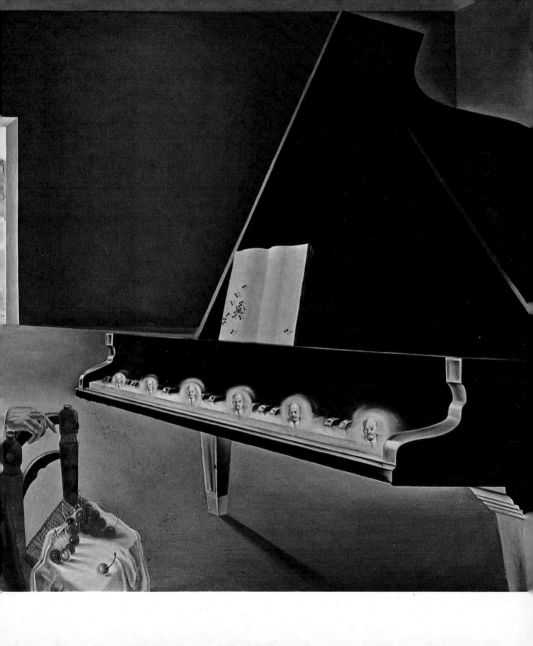

24   Symbole agnostique. 1932. Agnostic Symbol.

25
Moi à dix ans quand
j'étais enfant-sauterelle
1933
Myself at the Age of Ten
when I was Grasshopper Child

26   Méditation sur une harpe
1932-1934. Meditation on the Harp

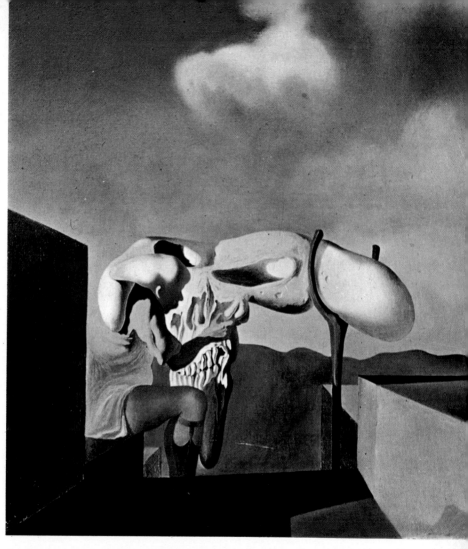

27 Bureaucrate moyen atmosphéricocéphale en train de traire une harpe crânienne.
1933. Average Atmospherocephalic Bureaucrat in the act of milking a Cranial Harp.

28
Naissance des
désirs liquides
1932
The Birth of
Liquid Desires

29   Le Sphinx de sucre. détail. 1933. Sugar Sphinx.

30 Le Spectre de Vermeer pouvant être utilisé comme table.
1934. The Ghost of Vermeer of Delft which can be used as a Table.

32
Vestiges ataviques
après la pluie
1934
Atavistic Vestiges
after the Rain

31   Le Sevrage du meuble-aliment
1934. The Weaning of Furniture-Nutrition

33
L'Angélus de Gala
1935
Portrait of Gala with
the "Angelus" of Millet

34　Réminiscence archéologique de l'Angélus de Millet
1933-1935. Archeological Reminiscence of Millet's Angelus

35   Construction molle avec des haricots bouillis. Paysage de guerre civile.
1936. Soft Construction with Boiled Beans. Premonition of Civil War.

37
L'Énigme de
Guillaume Tell
1934
The Enigma of
William Tell

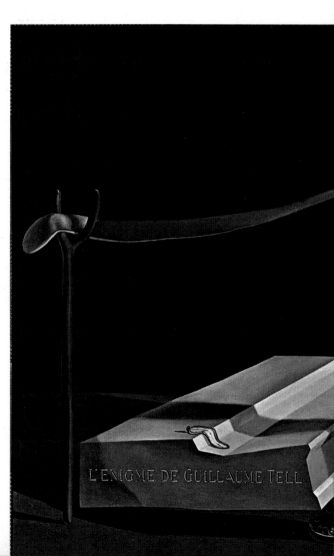

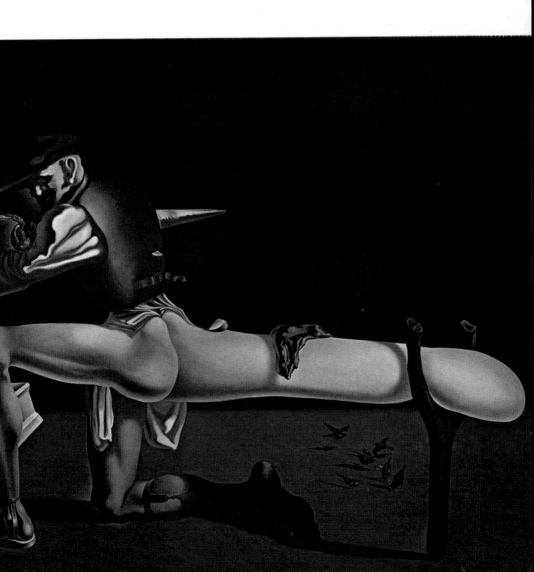

38   Image médiumnique paranoïaque. 1934. Paranoic-Astral Image.

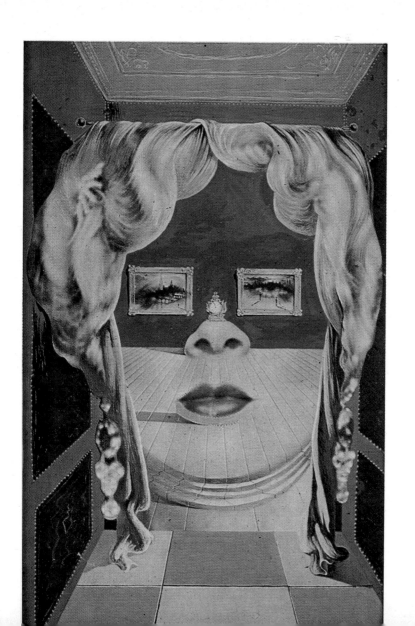

41   Le Sphinx de Barcelone. 1939. The Sphinx of Barcelona.

40
Portrait de Mae West
1934-1936

43
Crâne avec son
accessoire lyrique
1934
Skull with
its Lyric Appendage

42   Crâne atmosphérique sodomisant un piano à queue.
1934. Atmospheric Skull Sodomizing a Grand Piano.

44   45
Mémoire de la femme-enfant
ensemble et détail
1932
Memory of
the Child-Woman

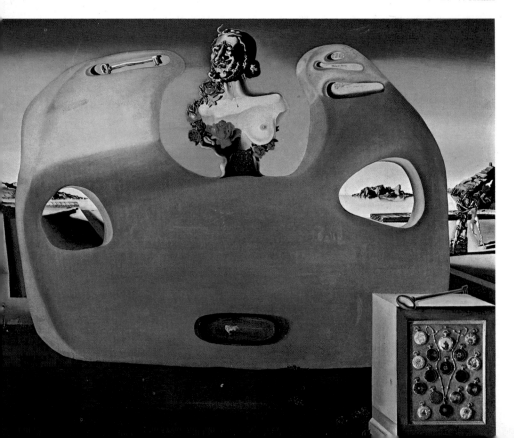

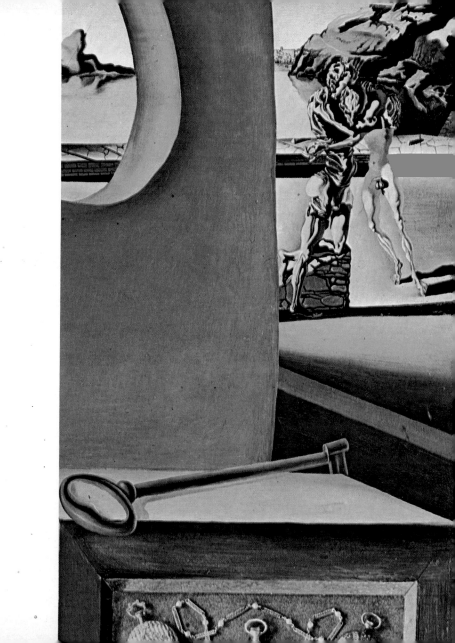

46   Femmes aux têtes de fleurs retrouvant sur la plage la peau d'un piano à queue.
1936. Three Young Surrealist Women Holding in their Arms the Skins of an Orchestra.

47   Plage enchantée avec trois grâces fluides.
1938. Enchanted Beach with Three Fluid Graces.

48
Araignée du soir espoir !
1940
Daddy Longlegs of the Evening... Hope!

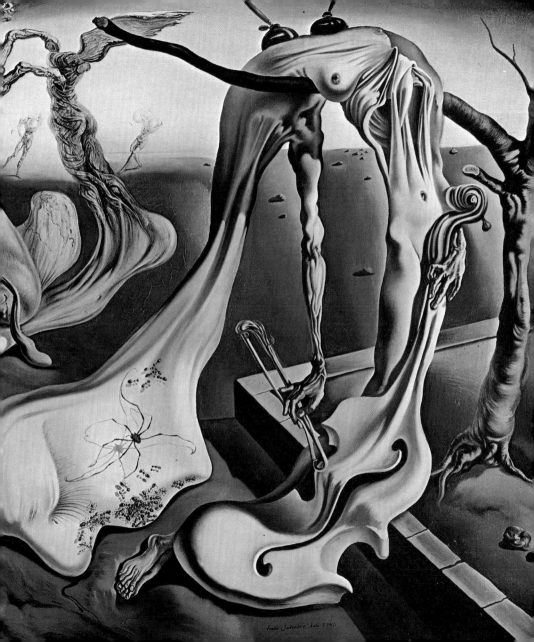

50
Le Buste invisible
de Voltaire
détail
1941
Disappearing Bust
of Voltaire

49   Marché d'esclaves avec le buste invisible de Voltaire.
1940 Slave Market with the Disappearing Bust of Voltaire.

51
Vieillesse, Adolescence, Enfance !
1940
Old Age, Adolescence, Infancy
(The Three Ages)

52   Téléphone dans un plat avec trois sardines grillées.
1939. Telephone in a Dish with Three Grilled Sardines at the End of September.

53
Croix nucléaire
1952
Nuclear Cross

54 Enfant géopolitique observant la naissance de l'homme nouveau.
    1943. Geopoliticus Child Watching the Birth of the New Man.

55   56
La Madone de Port Lligat
détail et ensemble
1950
The Madonna of Port Lligat

57 Paysage de Port Lligat. 1950. Landscape of Port Lligat.

58   L'Ange de Port Lligat. 1952. The Angel of Port Lligat.

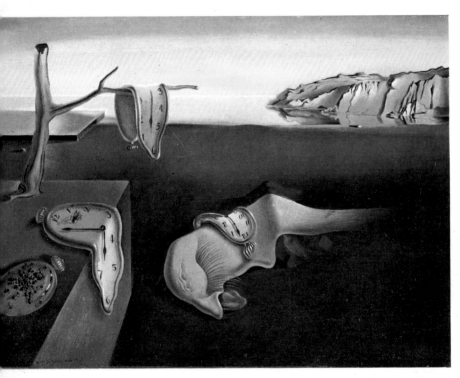

59
Persistance de la mémoire (les Montres molles)
1931. The Persistence of Memory

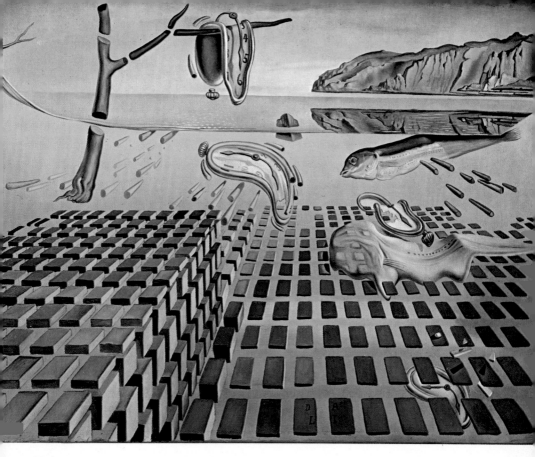

60
Le Chromosome d'un œil de poisson très coloré
entamant la désintégration de la persistance de la mémoire
1952-1954
The Disintegration of the Persistence of Memory

61 L'Homme à la tête d'hortensia. 1936. The Man with the Head of Blue Hortensias.

62   Le Spectre du sex-appeal. 1934. The Ghost of Sex-Appeal.

63 64
Écho antropomorphique
ensemble et détail
1948
Anthropomorphic Echo

65
La Cène
1955
The Last Supper

66
Jeune Vierge
autosodomisée par
les cornes de
sa propre chasteté
1954

67　Nature morte vivante. 1956. Still Life Fast Moving.

69 Vitesse maxima de la Vierge de Raphaël, 1954
The Top Speed of Raphael's Virgin

68   Dali ! Dali ! 1954

70 Titre inconnu. détail. 1950. Un Known Title.

71
Découverte de l'Amérique
par Christophe Colomb
détail
1958-1959
The Discovery of America
by Christopher Columbus

72 73
Découverte de l'Amérique
par Christophe Colomb
détails
1958-1959
The Discovery of America
by Christopher Columbus

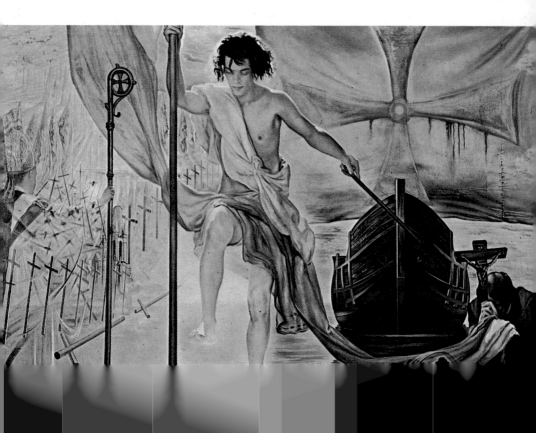

74
Découverte de l'Amérique
par Christophe Colomb
1958-1959
The Discovery of America
by Christopher Columbus

75
Velasquez peignant
l'Infante Marguerite
entourée des lumières
et des ombres de
sa propre gloire
1958
Velazquez Painting
the Infanta Margarita
with the lights
and Shadows of
his own Glory

76　Velasquez peignant l'Infante Marguerite (détail)
1958. Velazquez Painting the Infanta Margarita.

77 Velasquez peignant l'Infante Marguerite (détail)
1958. Velazquez Painting the Infanta Margarita.

81   82
Dionysos crachant l'image
complète de Cadaquès
détail et ensemble
1968

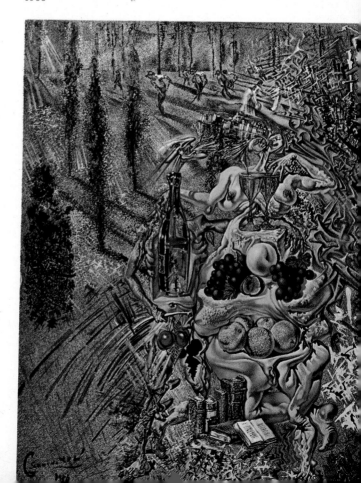

85   86
Toréador hallucinogène
détail et ensemble
1969-1970
The Hallucinogenic Toreador

87
Concile œcuménique
détail
1960
The Ecumenical Council